CGP are in the top division for Maths!

This CGP book quickly gets pupils up to speed with the Multiplication and Division skills they need for Year 2.

Each test only takes 10 minutes, so they're ideal for quick practice sessions — and we've carefully crafted each one to get more difficult as pupils build up their confidence.

We've even included step-by-step answers to every question — plus a handy chart to check progress too!

What CGP is all about

Our sole aim here at CGP is to produce the highest quality books — carefully written, immaculately presented and dangerously close to being funny.

Then we work our socks off to get them out to you — at the cheapest possible prices.

Published by CGP

Editors: Martha Bozic, Liam Dyer and Samuel Mann

With thanks to Gareth Mitchell and Ben Train for the proofreading.

With thanks to Jan Greenway for the copyright research.

ISBN: 978 1 78908 635 5

Graphics used throughout the book © www.edu-clips.com
Printed by Zenith Print & Packaging Ltd, Pontypridd.

Based on the classic CGP style created by Richard Parsons.

Text, design, layout and original illustrations © Coordination Group Publications Ltd. (CGP) 2020
All rights reserved.

Photocopying this book is not permitted, even if you have a CLA licence.
Extra copies are available from CGP with next day delivery • 0800 1712 712 • www.cgpbooks.co.uk

Contents

Test 1 2

Test 2 4

Test 3 6

Test 4 8

Test 5 10

Test 6 12

Test 7 14

Test 8 16

Test 9 18

Test 10 20

Test 11 22

Test 12 24

Answers 26

Progress Chart 30

How to Use this Book

- This book contains 12 tests, all geared towards improving your multiplication and division skills.

- Each test is out of 8 marks and should take about 10 minutes to complete.

- Each test starts with some warm-up questions to get you going and ends with a problem-solving question.

- The tests increase in difficulty as you go through the book.

- Answers and a Progress Chart can be found at the back of the book.

Test 1

Warm up

1. Use the pictures to help fill in the missing numbers.

   a) 2 × 2 = ...

   b) 3 × 2 = ...

   c) 4 × 2 = ...

   3 marks

2. Look at these pairs of boots.

   How many **pairs** of boots are there?

   .... pairs

   1 mark

   How many boots are there in **total**?

   .... boots

   1 mark

3. Match each number of pairs to the number of gloves in those pairs.

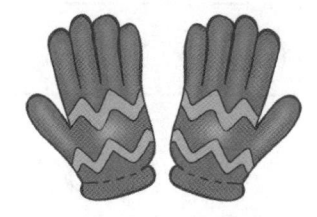

One has been done for you.

2 marks

4. Alison and Bakur share these apples **equally**.

How many apples do they each get?

.... apples

1 mark

END OF TEST

/ 8

Test 2

Warm up

1. Count up in steps of two to fill in the gaps.

   2   6   ....

   1 mark

2. Circle all the **odd** numbers.
   Use the pictures below to help you.

   3   6   8   10   11   12

   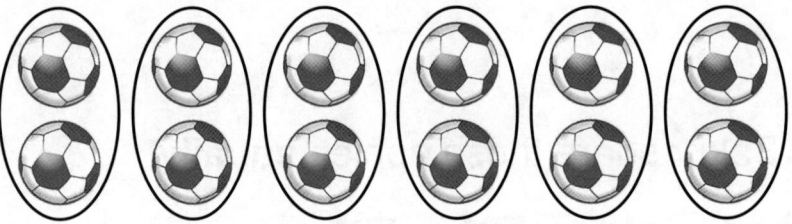

   1 mark

3. Work out these multiplications.

   $2 \times 3 =$ ....

   $5 \times 2 =$ ....

   2 marks

4. A starfish has 5 arms.

   Write the total number of arms the starfish have in each tank below.

    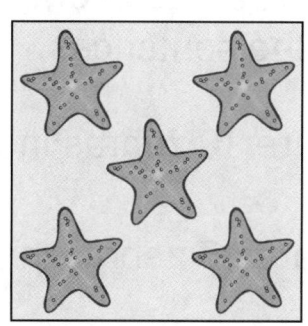

   .... arms   .... arms

   2 marks

5. Jada and Dean share 6 toffees and 4 lollies.
   They each get the same number of toffees and lollies.

   How many sweets do they each get?

   .... toffees and .... lollies

   2 marks

   END OF TEST

   / 8

Test 3

Warm up

1. There are 5 zebras in one group. Complete the sentences.

   a) There are 10 zebras in .... groups.

   b) There are 15 zebras in .... groups.

   2 marks

2. What number is:

   a) double 4? ....   b) half of 4? ....

   1 mark

3. Each of these butterflies has 5 spots.

   How many spots are on **six** butterflies?

   .... spots

   1 mark

4. Work out these multiplications.

   1 × 2 = ...   3 × 2 = ...

   6 × 2 = ...   8 × 2 = ...

   2 marks

5. The penguins below are in a group of 5.

   Complete the addition to find how many penguins there would be in 4 groups.

   ☐ + ☐ + ☐ + ☐ = ☐ penguins

   1 mark

   Complete the multiplication to find how many penguins there would be in 4 groups.

   ☐ × ☐ = ☐ penguins

   1 mark

   END OF TEST

   / 8

Test 4

Warm up

1. Circle all of the **even** numbers.
   Use the pictures below to help you.

   3   5   6   9   14   15

   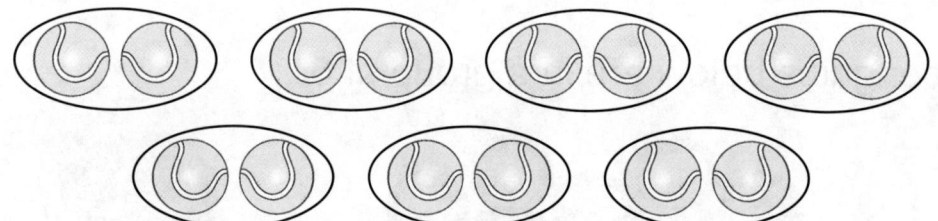

   1 mark

2. Work out these multiplications.

   a) 5 × 2 = ...   b) 10 × 2 = ...

   1 mark

3. Work out these divisions.

   8 ÷ 2 = ...   16 ÷ 2 = ...

   2 marks

4. Draw a line from each multiplication to its answer on the number line.

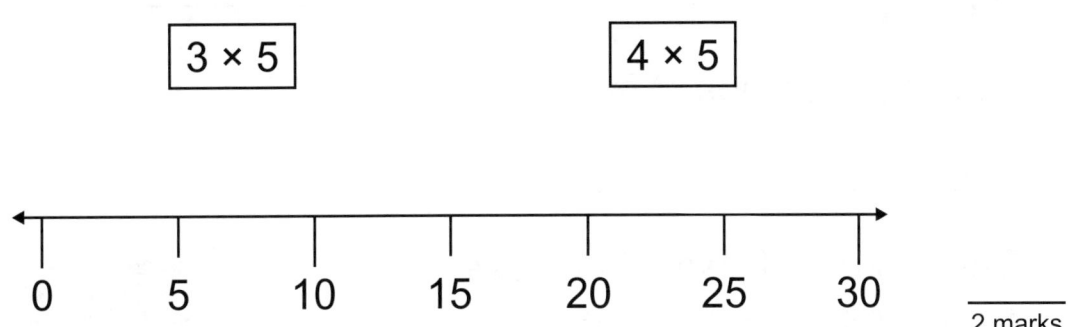

2 marks

5. Simone put **four groups of two** goldfish in her pond.

Which of these could **not** be her pond?
Put a cross in two ponds to show your answer.

2 marks

END OF TEST

/ 8

Test 5

Warm up

1. Count up in steps of five.

   5   10   ....

   1 mark

2. There are 10 flowers in a vase.
   Complete the sentences.

   a) There are .... flowers in 2 vases.

   b) There are 30 flowers in .... vases.

   2 marks

3. Work out these multiplications.

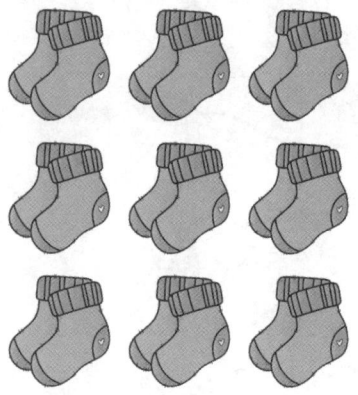 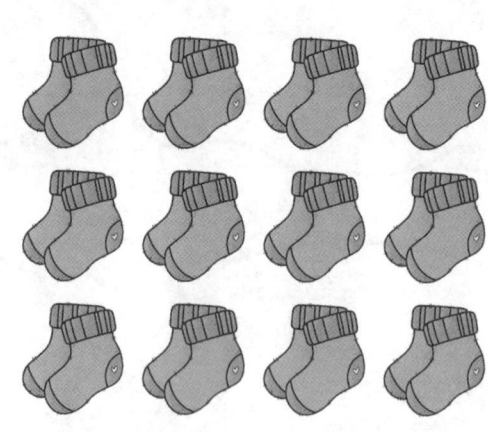

   9 × 2 = ...   12 × 2 = ...

   2 marks

4. Work out 4 × 10.

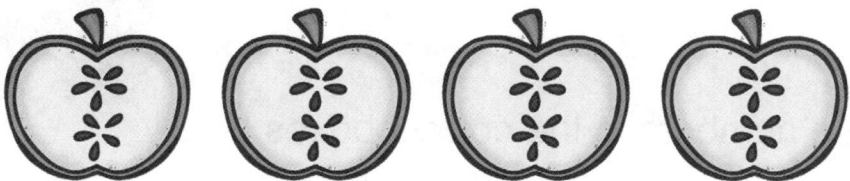

....

1 mark

5. James and Kelsey share 22 crayons equally.

How many crayons do they each get?

.... crayons

1 mark

James can draw 10 pictures in one hour.

How many pictures can he draw in **two hours**?

.... pictures

1 mark

END OF TEST

/ 8

Test 6

Warm up

1. Write these numbers in the correct boxes below.

   5   12   13   16   19

Even	Odd

   2 marks

2. Circle the calculation with the smallest answer.

   3 × 2   2 × 5   1 × 10

   1 mark

3. What is 15 divided by 5?

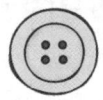 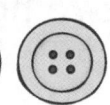  

....

1 mark

4. Fill in the boxes to find the total number of marbles.

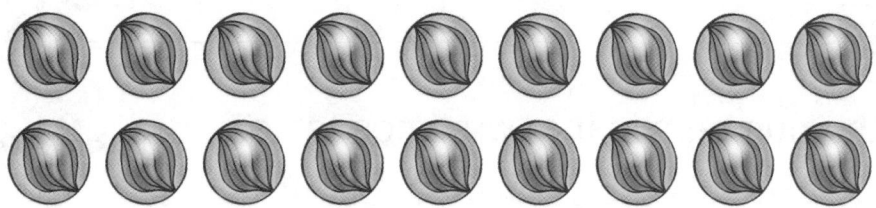

☐ × 2 = ☐ marbles

2 marks

5. Kim visits the park.
   She sees swans in pairs and ducks in groups of 5.

   How many swans are there in 7 pairs?

   .... swans

   1 mark

   How many ducks are there in 10 groups?

   .... ducks

   1 mark

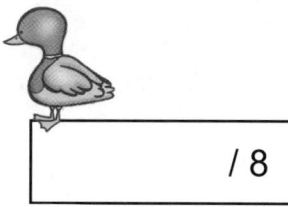

END OF TEST

/ 8

Test 7

Warm up

1. Circle the numbers in the two times table.

    4   9   11   14   16

    1 mark

2. Work out the answers to these divisions.

   a) 10 ÷ 2 = ...   b) 10 ÷ 5 = ...

   1 mark

3. There are 5 ladybirds on each leaf of a tree.

   How many ladybirds are there on 6 leaves?

   .... ladybirds

   1 mark

   How many ladybirds are there on 8 leaves?

   .... ladybirds

   1 mark

4. Complete these calculations.

10 × 2 = ...   7 × 2 = ...

11 × 2 = ...   9 × 2 = ...

2 marks

5. Carrots are sold in bags of five.

Mei buys **more than three** bags of carrots.

How many carrots could she have bought in **total**? Circle **all** of the correct options.

2   10   18   20

21   28   32   35

2 marks

END OF TEST

/ 8

Test 8

Warm up

1. Fill in the missing numbers in the five times table.

   25 .... 35 40 50

   1 mark

2. Draw lines to join the calculations which are the same.

20 × 2		five times twenty
20 ÷ 2		half of twenty
20 × 5		double twenty

   1 mark

3. Look at the list below.

   21 24 26 29 32 35

   Write all the even numbers from the list that are **less than 30**.

   ....
   2 marks

4. The number machines below take a number and multiply it by 10.

   Fill in the missing numbers.

   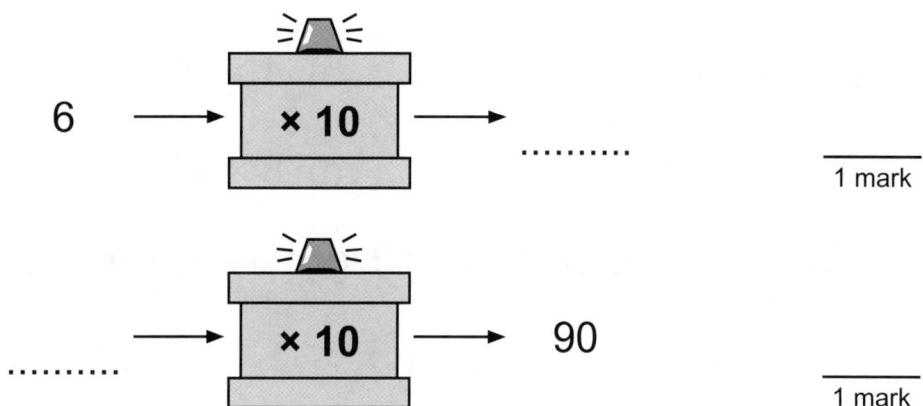

   1 mark

   1 mark

5. There are four green and five red balls in a bag. Johnny buys five bags of balls.

   How many balls does he buy altogether?

   .... balls

   2 marks

   END OF TEST

   / 8

Test 9

Warm up

1. Complete these multiplications.

   a) 2 × 10 = ...   b) 4 × 10 = ...

   c) 6 × 10 = ...   d) 8 × 10 = ...

   2 marks

2. Circle the division with the biggest answer.

   20 ÷ 5   20 ÷ 2   20 ÷ 10

   1 mark

3. Look at the clock face below.
   The **big hand** moves clockwise to point to **6**.

   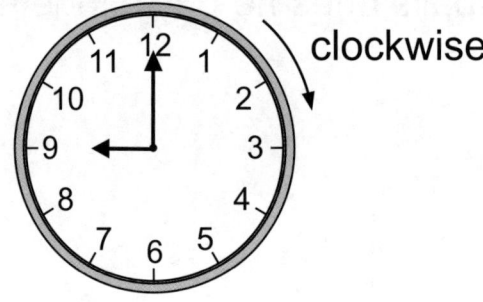

   Fill in the boxes to show how long this takes.

   ☐ × 5 minutes = ☐ minutes

   1 mark

4. Put ×, ÷ or = in each box to complete these calculations.

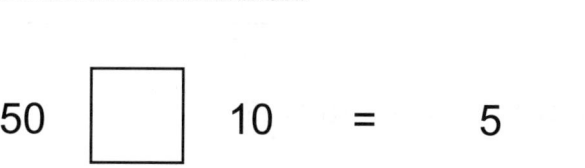

50 ☐ 10 = 5

12 ☐ 2 ☐ 24

2 marks

5. Bilal and Hannah are playing a game.

A treasure card is worth 2 points.
Bilal has 6 treasure cards.

Tick the calculations that give his score.

2 + 2 + 2 + 2 + 2 + 2 ☐   6 + 2 ☐

2 × 2 × 2 × 2 × 2 × 2 ☐   6 × 2 ☐

2 marks

END OF TEST   / 8

Test 10

Warm up

1. Work out these multiplications.

   a) 7 × 2 = ...   b) 4 × 5 = ...

   1 mark

2. Cross out two divisions that are wrong.

   | 20 ÷ 5 = 4 | | 30 ÷ 10 = 3 |

   | 10 ÷ 3 = 30 | | 5 ÷ 4 = 20 |

   1 mark

3. Complete the calculations below.
   Use each number from the box once.

   | 5   10   50   45 |

   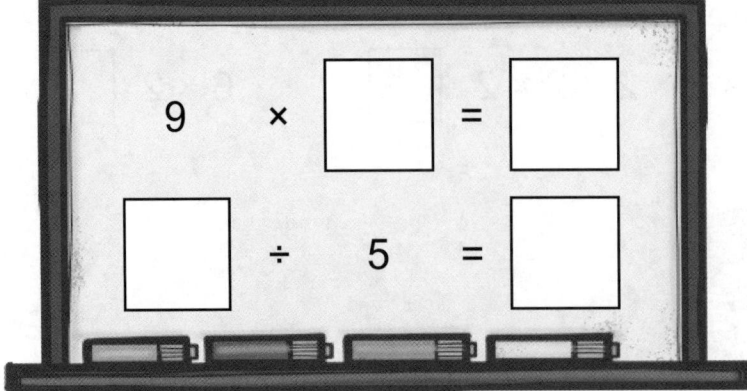

   9 × ☐ = ☐

   ☐ ÷ 5 = ☐

   2 marks

4. Sue makes 8 rows of 5 shells.

   Write a multiplication to work out the total number of shells.

   .... _____
   1 mark

   Ore makes 10 equal rows using 60 shells.

   Write a division to work out the number of shells in each row.

   .... _____
   1 mark

5. Andy has two pizzas. He cuts each pizza into six slices and gives away four slices to a friend.

   How many slices does Andy have left?

   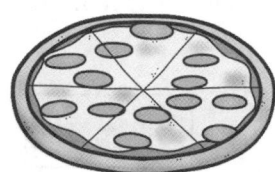

   .... slices _____
   2 marks

   END OF TEST

   / 8

Test 11

Warm up

1. Circle all the numbers in the five times table.

   10   18   25   30   41   46

   1 mark

2. Tick the correct box next to each number sentence.

   a) | 2 × 4 = 4 × 2 | True ☐   False ☐

   b) | 1 × 5 = 2 × 3 | True ☐   False ☐

   c) | 10 ÷ 2 = 2 ÷ 10 | True ☐   False ☐

   d) | 20 ÷ 5 = 8 ÷ 2 | True ☐   False ☐

   2 marks

3. Join each calculation to the correct answer.

   | 80 ÷ 10 | | 1 × 10 | | 90 ÷ 10 | | 8 × 10 |

    80    9    10    8

   2 marks

4. Make two **different** number sentences.
   Use the numbers from the box.

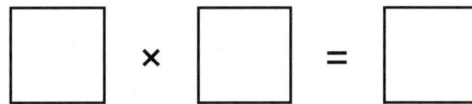

☐ × ☐ = ☐

☐ × ☐ = ☐

1 mark

5. A shop sells water bottles for £3 each.
   A bag costs £1 extra.
   Emma buys five water bottles and a bag.

   How much does she spend in total?

£..................

2 marks

END OF TEST

/ 8

Test 12

Warm up

1. Write each addition as a multiplication.

   a) 5 + 5 + 5 = ...

   b) 3 + 3 + 3 + 3 + 3 = ...

   1 mark

2. Join each calculation to its missing number.

? × 2 = 14		4
30 ÷ ? = 6		5
? × 10 = 40		6
12 ÷ 2 = ?		7

   2 marks

3. Complete the multiplication table.

×	2	3	....	....	11
10	20	....	50	70	....

   2 marks

4. Write ×, ÷ or = in each box to complete the number sentence.

fourteen ÷ two ☐ seven

twenty five = five ☐ five

1 mark

5. Five children are playing a game with some tiles. The amount of each tile is shown below.

20 stripy tiles   15 spotty tiles

 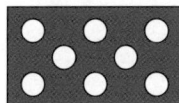

All tiles are shared equally between the children.

How many tiles does each child get?

.... tiles

2 marks

END OF TEST

/ 8

Answers

Test 1 – pages 2-3

1. a) 4   b) 6   c) 8
   (**1 mark for each correct answer**)
2. 5 pairs (**1 mark**)
   5 × 2 = 10 boots (**1 mark**)
3.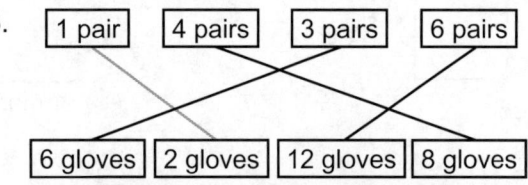
   (**2 marks for all three lines drawn correctly, otherwise 1 mark for at least one correct line**)
4. 8 apples shared between 2 people is 8 ÷ 2 = 4 apples. (**1 mark**)

Test 2 – pages 4-5

1. 2, 4, 6, 8, 10 (**1 mark**)
2. 3 and 11 should be circled.
   (**1 mark for both correct**)
3. 2 × 3 = 6 (**1 mark**)
   5 × 2 = 10 (**1 mark**)
4. There are 3 starfish in the first tank. They have 3 × 5 = 15 arms. (**1 mark**)
   There are 5 starfish in the second tank. They have 5 × 5 = 25 arms. (**1 mark**)
5. 6 toffees shared between 2 people is 6 ÷ 2 = 3 and 4 lollies shared between 2 people is 4 ÷ 2 = 2, so they each get 3 toffees and 2 lollies.
   (**1 mark for the correct number of lollies. 1 mark for the correct number of toffees**)

Test 3 – pages 6-7

1. a) There are 10 zebras in 2 groups.
   b) There are 15 zebras in 3 groups.
   (**1 mark for each correct answer**)
2. a) Double 4 is 8   b) Half of 4 is 2
   (**1 mark for both correct**)
3. 6 × 5 = 30 spots (**1 mark**)
4. 1 × 2 = 2   3 × 2 = 6
   6 × 2 = 12   8 × 2 = 16
   (**2 marks for all four correct answers, otherwise 1 mark for at least two correct answers**)
5. 5 + 5 + 5 + 5 = 20 penguins (**1 mark**)
   4 × 5 = 20 penguins
   (or 5 × 4 = 20 penguins) (**1 mark**)

Test 4 – pages 8-9

1. 6 and 14 should be circled.
   (**1 mark for both correct**)
2. a) 10   b) 20
   (**1 mark for both correct**)
3. 8 ÷ 2 = 4 (**1 mark**)
   16 ÷ 2 = 8 (**1 mark**)
4.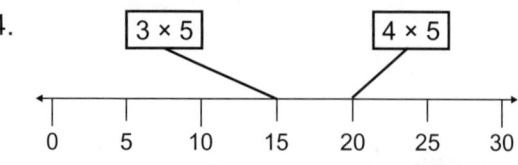
   (**1 mark for each correct line drawn**)

5. 4 × 2 = 8, so a cross should be put in the ponds that don't have 8 fish:

(**1 mark for each correct pond**)

Test 5 – pages 10-11

1. 5, 10, 15, 20, 25 (**1 mark**)
2. a) There are 20 flowers in 2 vases.
   b) There are 30 flowers in 3 vases.
   (**1 mark for each correct answer**)
3. 9 × 2 = 18 (**1 mark**)
   12 × 2 = 24 (**1 mark**)
4. 4 × 10 = 40 (**1 mark**)
5. They each get 22 ÷ 2 = 11 crayons. (**1 mark**)
   He can draw 10 pictures in one hour, so he can draw 2 × 10 = 20 pictures in two hours. (**1 mark**)

Test 6 – pages 12-13

1. 12 and 16 should be in the 'Even' box. 5, 13 and 19 should be in the 'Odd' box.
   (**2 marks for all numbers in the correct boxes, otherwise 1 mark for at least two numbers in the correct boxes and no more than one number in an incorrect box**)

2. 3 × 2 = 6, 2 × 5 = 10 and 1 × 10 = 10, so 3 × 2 should be circled. (**1 mark**)
3. 15 ÷ 5 = 3 (**1 mark**)
4. There are 9 marbles on each row and there are 2 rows, so the multiplication should be:
   9 × 2 = 18 marbles
   (**1 mark for each correct missing number**)
5. 7 × 2 = 14 swans (**1 mark**)
   10 × 5 = 50 ducks (**1 mark**)

Test 7 – pages 14-15

1. 4, 14 and 16 should be circled.
   (**1 mark for all three correct**)
2. a) 5   b) 2
   (**1 mark for both correct**)
3. 6 × 5 = 30 ladybirds (**1 mark**)
   8 × 5 = 40 ladybirds (**1 mark**)
4. 10 × 2 = 20   7 × 2 = 14
   11 × 2 = 22   9 × 2 = 18
   (**2 marks for all four correct, otherwise 1 mark for at least two correct**)
5. 4 bags have 4 × 5 = 20 carrots, 5 bags have 5 × 5 = 25 carrots, and so on. She must have bought a number of carrots in the 5 times table (larger than 15), so 20 and 35 should be circled.
   (**2 marks for both correct numbers circled and no others, otherwise 1 mark for one correct number circled and no more than one incorrect number circled**)

Test 8 – pages 16-17

1. 25, 30, 35, 40, 45, 50
   (1 mark for both correct)
2.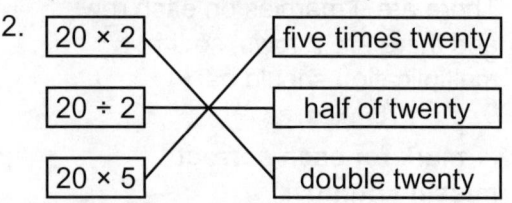
   (1 mark for all three lines drawn correctly)
3. 24 and 26
   (2 marks for both correct, otherwise 1 mark for one correct number and no more than one incorrect number)
4. 6 → ×10 → 60 **(1 mark)**

   9 → ×10 → 90 **(1 mark)**
5. There are 4 + 5 = 9 balls in a bag. So Johnny buys 9 × 5 = 45 balls altogether.
   (2 marks for the correct answer, otherwise 1 mark for a correct method)

Test 9 – pages 18-19

1. a) 20   b) 40
   c) 60   d) 80
   (2 marks for all four correct, otherwise 1 mark for at least two correct)
2. 20 ÷ 5 = 4, 20 ÷ 2 = 10 and 20 ÷ 10 = 2, so 20 ÷ 2 should be circled. **(1 mark)**
3. Each division on a clock is worth 5 minutes. So the big hand takes 6 × 5 minutes = 30 minutes.
   (1 mark)
4. 50 ÷ 10 = 5
   12 × 2 = 24
   (2 marks for all three correct, otherwise 1 mark for two correct)
5. He has 6 treasure cards, so he has '6 lots of 2 points'. So the calculations that should be ticked are:
   2 + 2 + 2 + 2 + 2 + 2 and 6 × 2.
   (2 marks for both correctly ticked, otherwise 1 mark for one correctly ticked and no more than one incorrectly ticked)

Test 10 – pages 20-21

1. a) 14   b) 20
   (1 mark for both correct)
2. 10 ÷ 3 = 30 and 5 ÷ 4 = 20 should be crossed out.
   (1 mark for both correct)
3. 9 × 5 = 45
   50 ÷ 5 = 10
   (2 marks for all four correct, otherwise 1 mark for at least two correct)
4. 8 × 5 = 40 (or 5 × 8 = 40) **(1 mark)**
   60 ÷ 10 = 6 **(1 mark)**
5. There are 6 × 2 = 12 slices in total. He gives away 4 slices, so he has 12 − 4 = 8 slices left.
   (2 marks for the correct answer, otherwise 1 mark for a correct method)

Answers

Test 11 – pages 22-23

1. 10, 25 and 30 should be circled.
   (1 mark for all three correct)
2. a) True b) False
   c) False d) True
   (2 marks for all four correct, otherwise 1 mark for at least two correct)
3.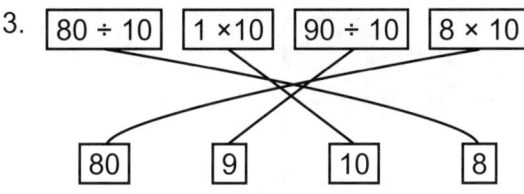
   (2 marks for all four lines drawn correctly, otherwise 1 mark for at least two correct lines)
4. 5 × 12 = 60
   12 × 5 = 60
   (1 mark for both correct)
5. 5 water bottles cost £3 × 5 = £15. A bag costs £1, so Emma spends £15 + £1 = £16 in total.
   (2 marks for the correct answer, otherwise 1 mark for a correct method)

Test 12 – pages 24-25

1. a) 3 × 5 (or 5 × 3)
   b) 5 × 3 (or 3 × 5)
   (1 mark for both correct)
2.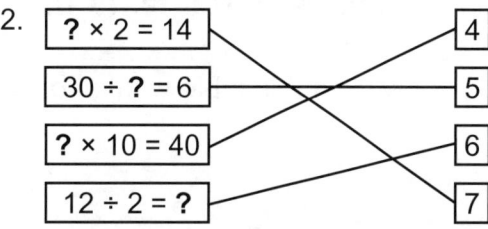
   (2 marks for all four lines drawn correctly, otherwise 1 mark for at least two correct lines)
3.

×	2	3	5	7	11
10	20	30	50	70	110

   (2 marks for all four correct numbers, otherwise 1 mark for at least two correct numbers)
4. fourteen ÷ two = seven
   twenty five = five × five
   (1 mark for both correct)
5. There are 20 + 15 = 35 tiles in total. They are shared between 5 children, so each child gets 35 ÷ 5 = 7 tiles.
   (2 marks for the correct answer, otherwise 1 mark for a correct method)

Progress Chart

That's all the tests in the book done — nice one!

Now fill in this table with all of your scores and see how you got on.

	Score
Test 1	
Test 2	
Test 3	
Test 4	
Test 5	
Test 6	
Test 7	
Test 8	
Test 9	
Test 10	
Test 11	
Test 12